D0635934

MEDIKIDZ EXPLAIN SLEEP APNEA

rosen publishing's
rosen central®
New York

Dr. Kim Chilman-Blair and Shawn deLoache

Medical content reviewed for accuracy by Dr. Paul Gringras and Dr. David Rapoport

This edition published in 2011 by:

The Rosen Publishing Group, Inc.
29 East 21st Street
New York, NY 10010

Additional end matter copyright © 2011 by The Rosen Publishing Group, Inc.

Library of Congress Cataloging-in-Publication Data

Chilman-Blair, Kim.
Medikidz explain sleep apnea / Kim Chilman-Blair and Shawn deLoache ; medical content reviewed for accuracy by Paul Gringras and David Rapoport.
    p. cm. — (Superheroes on a medical mission)
Includes bibliographical references and index.
ISBN 978-1-4358-9459-4 (library binding) — ISBN 978-1-4488-1841-9 (pbk.) — ISBN 978-1-4488-1842-6 (6-pack)
1. Sleep apnea syndromes—Comic books, strips, etc—Juvenile literature. I. Deloache, Shawn. II. Title.
RC737.5C55 2011
616.2'09—dc22
                            2010002554

Manufactured in China

CPSIA Compliance Information: Batch #MS0102YA: For further information, contact Rosen Publishing, New York, New York, at 1-800-237-9932.

THE WINDPIPE SPLITS INTO THE *LEFT MAIN BRONCHUS* AND *RIGHT MAIN BRONCHUS*...

...EACH ONE DIVIDES INTO SMALLER TUBES, CALLED *BRONCHI*, WHICH EVENTUALLY DIVIDE INTO SMALLER AND SMALLER TUBES, CALLED *BRONCHIOLES.*

← WINDPIPE

← LEFT MAIN BRONCHUS

← BRONCHI

← BRONCHIOLES

← ALVEOLI

ALVEOLI ARE THE TINY SACS OF AIR THAT MAKE UP YOUR LUNGS.

IT'S THE *END OF THE LINE* FOR THE *AIR* IN YOUR LUNGS.

LOOK HOW THE *UPPER AIRWAY* HAS BEEN BLOCKED OFF.

NO AIR CAN GET THROUGH TO THE *LUNGS...*

OXYGEN MOLECULE

LIKE A BIG SPONGE!...

BUT FULL OF AIR.

LOOK, GUYS... *THE JET!!*

GASTRO MUST HAVE SURVIVED THE FALL...

...AND GONE LOOKING FOR...

...US!?!?

NO, SOMETHING TO EAT!

BUT THE ONLY THING I COULD FIND TO EAT AROUND HERE IS *OXYGEN!!!!*

YOUR CELLS NEED OXYGEN TO STAY ALIVE.

YOU SAVED MY JET!

OLD CHUM... OLD PAL!

SO...HOW DOES THE *OXYGEN* GET FROM *HERE*...TO THE *CELLS?*

BY HITCHING A RIDE WITH THE *RED BLOOD CELLS*...

THE OXYGEN SEEPS THROUGH THE VERY *THIN* WALLS OF THE ALVEOLI...

...AND INTO THE BLOODSTREAM.

LET'S TAKE A CLOSER LOOK!

CLICK!!!

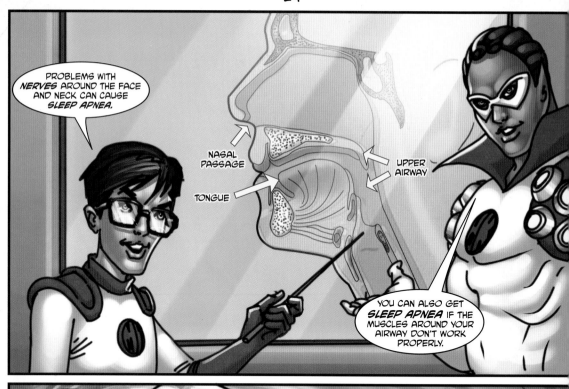

SLEEP APNEA IS MORE COMMON IN OLDER KIDS WHO ARE OVERWEIGHT...

STOMACH, OLD FRIEND, MAYBE IT'S TIME TO LOSE A FEW POUNDS...

HOW COME?

MORE FAT ON YOUR *THROAT* AND *BEHIND YOUR TONSILS* MAKES YOUR AIRWAY NARROWER...

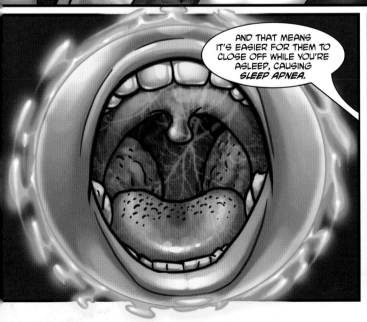

AND THAT MEANS IT'S EASIER FOR THEM TO CLOSE OFF WHILE YOU'RE ASLEEP, CAUSING *SLEEP APNEA.*

IN OLDER KIDS, HEALTHY DIET AND REGULAR EXERCISE HELP TO KEEP *SLEEP APNEA* AT BAY!

LOOK ON THE BRIGHT SIDE, AT LEAST YOU DIDN'T WET THE BED...

...YET.

WET THE BED?!?! ARE YOU KIDDING ME!

GAH!

WELL, IT'S NOBODY'S FAVORITE TOPIC FOR DINNER CONVERSATION, BUT *SLEEP APNEA* CAN SOMETIMES CAUSE BED-WETTING.

I'M GOING TO NEED SOME NEW PANTS.

BUT DON'T WORRY! TREATING SLEEP APNEA CAN HELP WITH THAT.

GLOSSARY

ADENOIDS A MASS OF TISSUE LOCATED AT THE BACK OF THE NOSE AND THROAT THAT CAN RESTRICT BREATHING IF IT IS ENLARGED.

ALVEOLI TINY AIR SACS IN THE LUNGS WHERE GASES ARE EXCHANGED.

ANTICIPATE TO EXPECT SOMETHING; TO THINK OR BE FAIRLY CERTAIN THAT SOMETHING WILL HAPPEN.

BRAIN STEM A STRUCTURE OF THE BRAIN THAT CONTROLS INTERNAL ORGANS AND THE BASIC BODY FUNCTIONS.

BRONCHIOLES NARROW TUBES INSIDE THE LUNGS THAT BRANCH OFF THE MAIN AIR PASSAGES' BRONCHI.

BRONCHI (SINGULAR, BRONCHUS) TWO LARGE TUBES THAT BRANCH OFF THE WINDPIPE (TRACHEA) INTO THE LUNGS.

COLLAPSE TO DEFLATE, TO FOLD UP, OR TO BECOME FLAT FROM LACK OF PRESSURE OR LOSS OF AIR; TO FALL DOWN.

CONTINUOUS POSITIVE AIRWAY PRESSURE (CPAP) A TREATMENT FOR SLEEP APNEA IN WHICH A MASKLIKE DEVICE BLOWS A GENTLE STREAM OF AIR INTO THE NOSE DURING SLEEP TO HELP KEEP THE AIRWAY OPEN.

HYPERACTIVE UNUSUALLY ACTIVE, RESTLESS, AND LACKING THE ABILITY TO CONCENTRATE FOR ANY LENGTH OF TIME.

LUNGS IN AIR-BREATHING VERTEBRATES, THE PAIRED SPONGY RESPIRATORY ORGANS THAT ARE LOCATED INSIDE THE RIB CAGE AND THAT TRANSFER OXYGEN INTO THE BLOOD AND REMOVE CARBON DIOXIDE FROM IT.

MANDIBULAR ADVANCEMENT DEVICE A DEVICE USED IN THE MOUTH TO HELP HOLD THE LOWER JAW (MANDIBLE) FORWARD. THE MOST COMMON TYPE IS A MOUTH GUARD THAT HOLDS THE LOWER JAW IN PLACE SO THAT THE TONGUE CANNOT FALL TO THE BACK OF THE THROAT TO CAUSE AN OBSTRUCTION.

NERVES A BUNDLE OF FIBERS THAT FORM A NETWORK AND TRANSMIT MESSAGES IN THE FORM OF IMPULSES BETWEEN THE BRAIN OR SPINAL CORD AND THE BODY'S ORGANS.

NEURON A CELL OF THE NERVOUS SYSTEM THAT IS SPECIALIZED TO CARRY "MESSAGES" TO AND FROM THE BRAIN TO THE OTHER PARTS OF THE BODY.

OXIMETRY A PROCEDURE THAT USES AN OXIMETER, AN
    INSTRUMENT THAT MEASURES THE AMOUNT OF
    OXYGEN IN THE BLOOD. THE TEST IS USED IN
    THE EVALUATION OF CONDITIONS THAT CAN AFFECT A
    PERSON'S HEART AND LUNGS.
OXYGEN A COLORLESS ODORLESS GAS THAT IS THE
    MOST ABUNDANT ELEMENT AND IS VITAL FOR PLANT
    AND ANIMAL RESPIRATION.
RED BLOOD CELLS CELLS THAT CARRY OXYGEN THROUGH
    THE BODY.
SLEEP APNEA A CONDITION IN WHICH A PERSON STOPS
    BREATHING PERIODICALLY DURING SLEEP.
SNORING BREATHING NOISILY WHILE ASLEEP BECAUSE
    OF VIBRATIONS TOWARD THE BACK OF THE ROOF OF
    THE MOUTH.
STAT IMMEDIATELY; URGENT.
TONSILS TWO SMALL OVAL MASSES OF TISSUE, ONE
    ON EACH SIDE OF THE BACK OF THE MOUTH, THAT
    ARE IMPORTANT FOR THE BODY'S IMMUNE SYSTEM.
WINDPIPE ALSO CALLED THE TRACHEA; THE TUBE IN THE
    BODY THAT CONDUCTS AIR FROM THE THROAT TO THE
    BRONCHI.

FOR MORE INFORMATION

AMERICAN ACADEMY OF SLEEP MEDICINE
6301 BANDEL ROAD, SUITE 101
ROCHESTER, MN 55901
(507) 287-6006
WEB SITE: HTTP://WWW.AASMNET.ORG
THE AMERICAN ACADEMY OF SLEEP MEDICINE INCREASES
        AWARENESS OF SLEEP DISORDERS IN PUBLIC AND
        PROFESSIONAL COMMUNITIES.

AMERICAN SLEEP APNEA ASSOCIATION
1424 K STREET NW, SUITE 302
WASHINGTON, DC 20005
WEB SITE: HTTP://WWW.SLEEPAPNEA.ORG
(202) 293-3650
THIS ASSOCIATION WORKS TO REDUCE PROBLEMS
        STEMMING FROM SLEEP APNEA AND TO HELP PEOPLE
        WITH SLEEP APNEA.

BETTER SLEEP COUNCIL
501 WYTHE STREET
ALEXANDRIA, VA 22314-1917
(703) 683-8371
WEB SITE: HTTP://WWW.BETTERSLEEP.ORG
THE BETTER SLEEP COUNCIL EDUCATES PEOPLE ABOUT
        THE IMPORTANCE OF SLEEP TO GOOD HEALTH AND
        QUALITY OF LIFE.

BETTER SLEEP COUNCIL CANADA
P.O. BOX 170
STREETSVILLE, ON L5M 2B8
CANADA
(416) 969-2809
WEB SITE: HTTP://WWW.BETTERSLEEP.CA
THE COUNCIL PROVIDES INFORMATION ABOUT SLEEP.

NATIONAL CENTER ON SLEEP DISORDERS RESEARCH
NATIONAL HEART, LUNG, AND BLOOD INSTITUTE
NHLBI INFORMATION CENTER
P.O. BOX 30105
BETHESDA, MD 20824
(301) 435-0199
WEB SITE: HTTP://WWW.NHLBI.NIH.GOV/ABOUT/NCSDR

THE CENTER PROMOTES, MAINTAINS, AND DISTRIBUTES
      INFORMATION ON SLEEP AND SLEEP DISORDERS.

NATIONAL HIGHWAY TRAFFIC SAFETY ADMINISTRATION
400 SEVENTH STREET SW
WASHINGTON, DC 20590
(888) 327-4236
WEB SITE: HTTP://WWW.HTTSA.GOV
THIS FEDERAL AGENCY IS CHARGED WITH SAVING LIVES,
      PREVENTING INJURIES, AND REDUCING TRAFFIC-
      RELATED ACCIDENTS. ITS WEB SITE HAS
      INFORMATION ON TEEN DRIVERS, INCLUDING SLEEPY
      DRIVERS.

NATIONAL SLEEP FOUNDATION
1522 K STREET NW, SUITE 500
WASHINGTON, DC 20005
(202) 347-3471
WEB SITE: HTTP://WWW.SLEEPFOUNDATION.ORG
THE NATIONAL SLEEP FOUNDATION WORKS TO IMPROVE
      UNDERSTANDING OF SLEEP AND SLEEP DISORDERS
      AND BY SUPPORTING SLEEP-RELATED EDUCATION,
      RESEARCH, AND ADVOCACY.

SLEEP/WAKE DISORDERS CANADA
3080 YONGE STREET, SUITE 5055
TORONTO, ON M4N 3N1
CANADA
(416) 483-9654
WEB SITE: HTTP://WWW.PSLGROUP.COM/DG/B538E.HTM
SLEEP/WAKE DISORDERS CANADA RAISES PUBLIC
      AWARENESS ABOUT SLEEP DISORDERS AND
      PROVIDES SUPPORT FOR THOSE WITH A SLEEP-WAKE
      DISORDER AND THEIR FAMILIES.

WEB SITES

DUE TO THE CHANGING NATURE OF INTERNET LINKS, ROSEN
PUBLISHING HAS DEVELOPED AN ONLINE LIST OF WEB SITES
RELATED TO THE SUBJECT OF THIS BOOK. THIS SITE IS
UPDATED REGULARLY. PLEASE USE THIS LINK TO ACCESS
THIS LIST:

HTTP://WWW.ROSENLINKS.COM/MED/SLEE

BAYER, LINDA. *SLEEP DISORDERS*. PHILADELPHIA, PA: CHELSEA HOUSE PUBLISHERS, 2001.

BRYNIE, FAITH HICKMAN. *101 QUESTIONS ABOUT SLEEP AND DREAMS THAT KEPT YOU AWAKE NIGHTS...UNTIL NOW.* MINNEAPOLIS, MN: TWENTIETH-CENTURY BOOKS, 2006.

COVEY, SEAN. *THE 7 HABITS OF HIGHLY EFFECTIVE TEENS PERSONAL WORKBOOK.* FOREST CITY, NC: FIRESIDE BOOKS, 2003.

ESHERICK, JOAN. *DEAD ON THEIR FEET: TEEN SLEEP DEPRIVATION AND ITS CONSEQUENCES.* PHILADELPHIA, PA: MASON CREST PUBLISHERS, 2005.

ESPELAND, PAMELA. *LIFE LISTS FOR TEENS: TIPS, STEPS, HINTS, AND HOW-TOS FOR GROWING UP, GETTING ALONG, LEARNING, AND HAVING FUN.* MINNEAPOLIS, MN: FREE SPIRIT PUBLISHING, 2003.

FOLDVERY-SCHAEFER, NANCY. *THE CLEVELAND CLINIC GUIDE TO SLEEP DISORDERS.* NEW YORK, NY: KAPLAN PUBLISHING, 2009.

FOX, ANNIE. *TOO STRESSED TO THINK? A TEEN GUIDE TO STAYING SANE WHEN LIFE MAKES YOU CRAZY.* MINNEAPOLIS, MN: FREE SPIRIT PUBLISHING, 2005.

HIPP, EARL. *FIGHTING INVISIBLE TIGERS: A STRESS MANAGEMENT GUIDE FOR TEENS.* MINNEAPOLIS, MN: FREE SPIRIT PUBLISHING, 2008.

HIRSHKOWITZ, MAX, AND PATRICIA B. SMITH. *SLEEP DISORDERS FOR DUMMIES.* HOBOKEN, NJ: WILEY PUBLISHING, INC., 2004.

MACGREGOR, ROB. *DREAM POWER FOR TEENS: WHAT YOUR DREAMS SAY ABOUT YOUR PAST, PRESENT, AND FUTURE.* CINCINNATI, OH: ADAMS MEDIA CORPORATION, 2005.

PETERSON, JUDY MONROE. *FREQUENTLY ASKED QUESTIONS ABOUT SLEEP AND SLEEP DEPRIVATION* (FAQ: TEEN LIFE). NEW YORK, NY: ROSEN PUBLISHING, 2010.

RENTZ, KRISTEN. *YOGANAP: RESTORATIVE POSES FOR DEEP RELAXATION.* CAMBRIDGE, MA: DA CAPO PRESS, 2005.

STEINLE, JASON. *UPLOAD EXPERIENCE: QUARTERLIFE SOLUTIONS FOR TEENS AND TWENTYSOMETHINGS.* EVERGREEN, CO: NASOJ PUBLICATIONS, 2005.

STEWART, GAIL B. *SLEEP DISORDERS.* SAN DIEGO, CA: LUCENT BOOKS, 2003.

TRUEIT, TRUDI STRAIN. *DREAMS AND SLEEP* (LIFE BALANCE). LONDON, ENGLAND: FRANKLIN WATTS, 2004.

ABOUT THE AUTHORS

DR. KIM CHILMAN-BLAIR IS A MEDICAL DOCTOR WITH TEN YEARS OF EXPERIENCE IN MEDICAL WRITING AND A PASSION FOR PROVIDING MEDICAL INFORMATION THAT MAKES CHILDREN WANT TO LEARN.

SHAWN DELOACHE HAS EARNED DEGREES IN PSYCHOLOGY AND CRIMINAL JUSTICE FROM THE UNIVERSITY OF GEORGIA IN ATHENS, GEORGIA. HE HAS WORKED WITH CHILDREN AS A COUNSELOR, TEACHER, AND MARTIAL ARTS INSTRUCTOR, AND CURRENTLY WORKS WITH SPECIAL NEEDS CHILDREN. HE MOVED TO NEW YORK IN 2006 TO PURSUE A WRITING CAREER IN NOVELS, TELEVISION, AND COMICS.